we wish you a
MERRY
CHRISTMAS
and a
HAPPY NEW YEAR

MAY THIS CHRISTMAS
be filled with
HAPPINESS
IN ALL That you DO
AND MAY THIS JOY
CONTINUE THE whole year THROUGH

HAPPY
HOLIDAYS

happy holidays

MERRY
CHRISTMAS
And
HAPPY NEW YEAR

Merry Christmas

HAVE YOURSELF A MERRY
CHRISTMAS
&
A HAPPY NEW YEAR

CHRISTMAS
HAPPY
HOLIDAYS
SEASON'S
GREETINGS
HAPPINESS
JOY
LOVE
HOPE
PEACE
MERRY
CHRISTMAS
HAPPY

MERRY
CHRISTMAS
AND A HAPPY NEW YEAR

Merry Christmas
PARTY

WISHING YOU A
MERRY
CHRISTMAS
AND
A HAPPY NEW YEAR

HAPPY
HOLLYDAYS

MERRY
CHRISTMAS
& HAPPY NEW YEAR

WISHING YOU A
Merry
CHRISTMAS
AND
A HAPPY NEW YEAR

Happy Holidays

MERRY CHRISTMAS
&
HAPPY
NEW
YEAR

WE WISH YOU A
MERRY
CHRISTMAS
AND A
HAPPY NEW YEAR

Merry Christmas

WE
WISH
YOU
A MERRY
CHRISTMAS

Season's
GREETINGS
from all of us